A Medley

Suganya Sundar

BookLeaf
Publishing

Presentation by *BookLeaf Publishing*

Web: www.bookleafpub.com

E-mail: info@bookleafpub.com

ISBN: 9789357617192

First edition 2022

*To all people who are afraid to try because
something won't turn out perfect.*

ACKNOWLEDGEMENT

Much obliged to BookLeaf Publishing for the opportunity. And grateful to all the wonderful people who had and have a hand in my existence.

PREFACE

Say you got on a short bus journey and an incredible idea popped up inside your mind but you are not skilled enough to convey them. But you tried anyways. At the end of the journey you just felt pleasant. No regrets.
Sometimes that's all we need at the end of the day.

?

How do you respect in full or in half?
Whom do you talk to, a loner or a crowd?
Where do you dwell in the present or past?
When do you start now or after?
Why do you wake up to shine or whine?
Whose opinion matters, yours or others?
Who are you when no one is watching?

Gratitude.

2

If you could eat you could serve
If you could eat you could cook
If you could eat you could grow
If you couldn't
Be greatful.

Myocardial infraction

Ivabradine on the horizon
Angioplasty a common term
Medicine discussing AI
Will all go in vain
As long as
Yes and nothing
Clog up the arteries.

Endangered species

Humans matching genetically
Remaining a species
Humans living practically
Remaining vulnerable
Humans liking to co-exist
Remaining endangered
Humans enthusiastic to rejoice
Remaining critically endangered
Humans willing to empathize
Remaining extinct in the wild
Humans wanting equality
Remaining extinct.

Miracles

5

Nostalgia of the past
Excitement of the future
Boredom of the present
Have blindfolded us
With miracles sauntering around
Without striking any sound

Life

Life is a toddler
Who governs us by
Murphy's laws.

One God

A god is a life-giver
A god is a life-saver
A god is supreme
A god is divine
A god is powerful
If I had to choose
One god
I would choose food.

Hunger.

To eat plants
Or
To eat meat
Is the not the right question,
To eat or not is.

Stars

The night skies astonished me
With millions of things
That shined and sparkled.
As a kid,
They left me curious and fascinated.
All I see now is
Scapegoats of convenient people.

Difficulty level : Hard

A small worm
Crossing a sidewalk.
A millipede
Crossing a concrete road.
A squirrel
Crossing a highway.
A human
Trying to remain good.

Sweet disaster.

A toddler is a recipe
That's made from scratch
The tantrum is
All the things put in
Unmeasured.

Countdown

Ten
In mind:
Do we really have to talk with them?
Nine
Heard that they are not that trustworthy.
Eight
Got an unlikely past.
Seven
We couldn't do it with anyone else
Six
Well that may not be the case
Five
It could happen to anyone
Four
They are not so bad after all
Three
There is no trouble between us
Two
Might be because of their situation
One
They are good people
Zero
Out loud: Hi how are you doing?

Trend

Piles of junk
Lies everywhere
No one cares
To pick it up
All we need
For a cleanup is
Put the junk
In trend and wait.

Coloring books

Distinguishes between
A child wild with imagination
And
An adult domesticated with instruction.

Sonder

15

A coffee shop bustling
Machines crackling and dripping
Each one leaving out
Wearing their own armor.

Bucket list

To climb into every page
Of the favorite books
To live with all
Of the favorite characters .

Sweet home

A rectangle box
Next to an electric pole
A vintage picture.

Formula

It must be an universal formula.
For success.
To hit hard at the rock bottom
For it does not contain any rocks line
But guess some kind of trampoline.

Skeletal equation

People suffering disease
Due to excess food
To
People suffering deficiency
Due to lack of food.

Baby girl.

We do not need
Wind chimes
For we had her.

Bird leaves

A caress
So tender
A feeling
So delicate
An epiphany
So true.